Pizza-zazz & Lotsa Pasta

Written by Kids Cooking Club®
Illustrated by Yancey Labat

Scholastic Inc.

New York   Toronto   London   Auckland   Sydney
Mexico City   New Delhi   Hong Kong   Buenos Aires

Designed by Peggy Gardner

ISBN 0-439-83187-3

Copyright © 2006 by Kids Cooking Club®, La Jolla, CA. All rights reserved.
Published by Scholastic Inc.

SCHOLASTIC and associated logos are trademarks and/or registered trademarks of Scholastic Inc.

Kids Cooking Club and associated logos are trademarks and/or registered trademarks of Kids Cooking Club, LLC.

12 11 10 9 8 7 6 5 4 3 2   6 7 8 9 10/0

Printed in China

First Scholastic printing, January 2006

Welcome To Kids Cooking Club®!

Come explore the kitchen with Kids Cooking Club where you're the chef! You'll discover that cooking is easy, fun, and best of all, you get to eat what you make! This cookbook includes some tasty treats, delicious pasta eats, and recipes that can't be beat!

Have you ever made a pizza face that looks like your little brother? What about a pizza that's made from brownie batter? There's even a pasta salad recipe that includes almost everything but the kitchen sink! The best thing about these recipes is that they are 100% kid-tested!

By being a member of KCC, you are in store for some good times and great memories that will remain long after the last ravioli is eaten. This is *your* cookbook, so use it often, try all the recipes, and most of all, have fun!

What Every Chef Needs To Know!

Safety Tips

◆ Read each recipe from start to finish before you begin.

◆ Wear an apron to keep your clothes clean. Wear short sleeves or roll them back. Tie back long hair.

◆ Wash your hands with soap and water *before* starting and *after* handling food, especially anything raw.

◆ Always use the oven and stove with grown-up supervision. They must also make sure the oven and stove are turned off when you're done cooking.

◆ Use dry oven mitts while handling anything hot!

◆ Turn off heat before removing a pot from the stove. Don't leave utensils inside pots while they are hot.

◆ Make sure all pot handles on the stove are turned away from you.

◆ Always use appliances with grown-up supervision.

- Never run or play roughhouse in the kitchen.

- Always use knives with grown-up supervision!

- Never hold the ingredient you are cutting in your hand. Keep it on the cutting board.

- Tuck non-cutting fingers under like a claw while using a knife.

- Keep a fire extinguisher handy in the kitchen and know how to use it.

Note to Grown-ups

All of the recipes in this book are designed for adult supervision **at all times**. Kids should never be left alone in the kitchen. There are many steps that grown-ups need to handle or supervise including, but not limited to, carrying hot pots and pans, working with sharp knives, operating appliances, overseeing kids at the stove, and ensuring that the oven is turned off after use.

 We have placed this icon next to those steps that will require your help.

Important Tools Chefs Need

Kids Cooking Club Apron: Protects clothes.

Measuring Cups & Spoons: For wet and dry ingredients.

Pizza Cutter and Server: When you're ready to eat.

Cheese Shakers: For Parmesan and Italian seasonings.

Mixing Bowls: Small, medium, and large ones.

Mixing Spoons: Large metal or wooden ones.

Pastry Brush: Or the end of a paper towel dipped in oil or butter.

Box Grater: For grating cheese.

Garlic Press: For making pizza and pasta.

Oven Mitts: Heavy mitts are best for small hands.

Sifter or Strainer: For dusting powdered sugar and separating eggs.

Colander: For draining pasta.

Whisk: Or a large fork.

Metal Tongs: For grabbing and turning hot foods.

Rolling pin: Large wooden ones are best for dough.

Knives: Small paring knife (with adult supervision).

To be a great chef, you need to be safe, have the right supplies, and speak the lingo! Check out these cool cooking terms:

Al Dente: Italian for "to the tooth". To boil pasta just enough so it retains a somewhat firm texture.

Chop: To cut into small pieces using a sharp knife.

Clean up: To leave the kitchen spic and span when finished.

Dice: To cut into small, even-size cubes.

Dust: To lightly sprinkle with flour or sugar.

Grate: To rub on a box grater and produce fine particles. Be sure to use a large enough piece of cheese so your fingers don't get close to the sharp holes.

Grease: To spread a thin layer of shortening or oil on a baking pan. Spray oil works well.

Knead: To make homemade dough soft and elastic. To do this, put dough on a lightly floured surface. Use the heels of both hands to push the dough away from yourself and then grab the far edge and fold it towards you. Repeat until dough is soft and not sticky.

Mince: To cut food into very small pieces; use a garlic press when available.

Pinch: The amount you can pick up between your thumb and pointer finger.

Proofing Yeast: Yeast is a type of plant that needs water, food, and warmth to grow. When you "proof" the yeast, you provide it with warm water, sugar (the food), and a warm place to grow.

Sauté: In French, sauté means, "to jump". To cook on stove in a small amount of fat or oil.

Seeded: To scrape out the membranes and seeds inside of bell peppers and chiles.

Separating Eggs: To separate the egg yolk from the white. To do this, either use an inexpensive egg separator or a small strainer. You can also put the whole egg in a small bowl and scoop out the yolk with a spoon.

Shred: To cut food into slivers or slender pieces, using a knife or shredder.

Simmer: To heat liquid just below boiling.

Slice: To start at one end and cut into thin, even pieces.

To Taste: Means to your liking.

Pizza Power!

Who doesn't love pizza? It's super yummy and it's so simple to make your own!

MAKES 6 KID-SIZE PIZZAS!

INGREDIENTS:

- ¼ teaspoon sugar
- ½ cup warm water
- 1 packet active dry yeast (¼ ounce)
- 1 cup warm water
- ¼ teaspoon salt
- 1½ tablespoons olive oil
- 4 cups unbleached flour
- Extra flour for dusting
- Extra olive oil for crusts
- Jar of favorite pizza sauce
- Toppings of choice (see pages 13-15)

TOOLS:

- ◆ Measuring spoons & cups
- ◆ Medium mixing bowl & fork
- ◆ Large mixing bowl & spoon
- ◆ Clean dishtowel
- ◆ Rolling pin
- ◆ Baking sheets
- ◆ Pastry brush
- ◆ Spatula
- ◆ Pizza cutter
- ◆ Pizza server

STEPS:

1. *Proof the yeast:* Put sugar and $\frac{1}{2}$ cup warm water in a medium bowl, then sprinkle yeast on top. Stir lightly with fork and let stand for 5 minutes or until bubbly (it stinks!). Add remaining 1 cup warm water, salt, and olive oil, and mix together.

2. Pour $3\frac{1}{2}$ cups flour into large bowl. Beat in the above yeast mixture with a large spoon. Use clean hands to mold dough into smooth, slightly sticky ball (if too sticky, add extra flour).

3. Dust a flat surface with flour and knead dough for about 10 minutes, or until the dough becomes soft and elastic.

4. Put dough back into large bowl and cover with dishtowel. Put in a warm place like a pantry to rise for 30–45 minutes. This is a good time to prepare the sauce and toppings you would like to use.

5. Preheat oven to 400° F.

(continued on page 11)

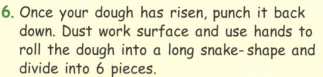

6. Once your dough has risen, punch it back down. Dust work surface and use hands to roll the dough into a long snake-shape and divide into 6 pieces.

7. Dust rolling pin and roll each piece of dough to make round crusts about 7–8 inches each. Brush off extra flour and place crusts on baking sheets.

 8. Brush the top side of each crust with a little olive oil. Put in oven and bake for about 5 minutes until lightly brown. Take crusts out of the oven and use a spatula to flip the crusts over so the slightly baked side is now on the bottom.

9. Spread sauce evenly on the non-baked side of the crust and start topping! But don't pile toppings too high or your pizza will not bake evenly.

 10. Bake for 10–15 minutes or until hot and bubbly. Let pizzas cool a bit so the toppings set. Cut and serve with pizza cutter and server.

Calzones

Here's another tasty option for your homemade pizza dough.

Tools:
♦ Rolling pin
♦ Baking sheet
♦ Pastry brush

Ingredients:

Flour for dusting

Homemade pizza dough or grocery store pizza dough

Fillings of choice (see pages 13-15)

Olive oil

Steps:

1. Preheat oven to 400° F.

2. Dust your work surface. For large calzones, roll $\frac{1}{2}$ of your pizza dough into a circle. For small calzones, roll smaller dough circles.

3. Put dough circles on baking sheet. Cover $\frac{1}{2}$ of the circle with your choice of fillings.

4. Fold the uncovered side over, then press the edges together. Lightly brush top with olive oil.

5. Bake for 15–20 minutes until golden brown and crusty. Cool a bit before eating.

Funny Face Pizza Party

Everyone likes their pizza a special way, so make it special by having your own "Funny Face Pizza Party." Use toppings to create funny faces. Make sure all ingredients are well washed and prepared before you start so you can let your creative juices flow!

Eyes & Eyebrows

- Pepperoni
- Salami
- Tomato slices
- Sliced olives
- Mushroom caps
- Asparagus
- Red, green, or yellow pepper slices
- Baby corn

Nose & Ears

- End cap of bell pepper
- Sliced mushrooms
- Cauliflower
- Broccoli spears
- Ring of bell pepper
- Salami chunk
- Slice of ham

Mouth & Teeth

- Pineapple ring
- Cheese slice or string cheese
- Tomato
- Zucchini cut into triangles
- Baby corn
- Olives
- Slice of sausage

Hair & Mustache

- Shredded cheese
- Shredded string cheese
- Shredded carrots
- Spinach
- Broccoli pieces
- Fresh parsley or other herbs

Top These!

Try one of these combinations and impress your friends with one fancy pie!

◆ **Hawaiian Pizza:** Sliced pineapple and ham.

◆ **Asian Cowboy Pizza:** Mandarin oranges and bacon.

◆ **Mexican Pizza:** Black beans, ground hamburger with Mexican seasoning, salsa, sliced olives, and jalapenos if you can handle the heat!

◆ **Stuffed Spinach Pizza Pie:** Make two pizza crusts. Put spinach, Parmesan cheese, sauce, and ham or turkey in the middle. Seal the edges and put slits in top crust.

◆ **Veggie Pizza Tart:** Press pizza dough into a tart pan. Spread bottom with pizza sauce. Top with mozzarella cheese, sliced red and green peppers, broccoli florets, sliced mushrooms, and sliced onions.

Mighty Secret Pizza Sauces

Shhh! Keep these mighty good pizza sauces a secret!

◆ **Pizzeria Tomato Sauce:** Mix 1 small can tomato paste with enough warm water to make a thin paste. Add 1 teaspoon chopped fresh garlic and 1 teaspoon dried oregano.

◆ **Pesto Sauce:** In a food processor or blender, chop 1 cup fresh basil leaves, 2 teaspoons salt, 1 clove peeled garlic, and 2 tablespoons pine nuts or walnuts until they form a puree (finely mashed to smooth consistency). Add $\frac{1}{4}$ cup olive oil and pulse several times, and then add $\frac{1}{4}$ cup fresh Parmesan or Romano cheese.

◆ **Margarita Style Sauce:** Mix together 8–10 diced Roma tomatoes, 3 chopped garlic cloves, $\frac{1}{2}$ cup shredded basil leaves, 1 teaspoon salt, and 2 teaspoons olive oil. Let the mixture marinate at least 1 hour before using.

◆ **Salsa Style Sauce:** Make like Margarita style above, but substitute cilantro for basil and add 2–3 grilled Serrano or jalapeno (if you like it HOT) chiles.

Sweet Pizzas!

Okay, these are really just great, big cookies! So top them with sweet toppings from our list or add a few of your own.

INGREDIENTS:

1 roll pre-made sugar cookie dough from a grocery store

Toppings of choice

TOOLS:

- ◆ Knife
- ◆ Cookie sheet, lightly greased
- ◆ Spatula

STEPS:

1. Preheat oven to 350° F.

2. Unwrap dough and slice into even pieces: 6 slices for large pizza cookies or 8 slices for medium-sized pizza cookies. Roll slices into balls and flatten using your hands on a lightly greased cookie sheet.

 3. Bake 10–15 minutes or until lightly browned. Remove from oven and let cool 2 minutes, then loosen with a spatula. Leave on sheet to cool before topping.

Sweet Pizza Topping Ideas

The great thing about dessert pizzas is that nothing is off limits if it tastes sweet (and Mom or Dad say it's okay).

◆ Fresh fruit like strawberries, blueberries, bananas, peaches, pineapple
◆ Real whipped cream
◆ Mini marshmallows
◆ Ice cream, tofutti, sherbet, frozen yogurt
◆ Chocolate, strawberry, or vanilla flavored syrups
◆ Flavored icings that come in a can
◆ Raisins, peanuts, walnuts
◆ Candy sprinkles, M&M's, jimmies
◆ Baking chips (white, semi-sweet, milk chocolate, or butterscotch)

The Big Brownie Pizza

Here's another great way to eat pizza! It's perfect for a class party or when you need to bring the treat after your soccer game. Personalize this pizza with your team name or a special message by making your own stencil as instructed.

INGREDIENTS:

1 package brownie mix
1 cup M&M's or other candy pieces
Powdered sugar

TOOLS:

- Mixing bowl & spoon
- 8–12 inch round pizza pan, lightly greased
- Spatula
- Plain white paper, scissors
- Sifter or strainer
- Toothpick

19

STEPS:

1. Preheat oven per directions on brownie package.
2. Prepare brownie mix per directions on package and spread mix evenly on pizza pan. Sprinkle the candy on top.
3. Bake until top is set and toothpick inserted comes out clean. Let cool before decorating.

PERSONALIZE YOUR BROWNIE PIZZA!

While the brownie is baking, make your own stencil to decorate the top with a personalized message.

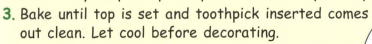

1. Using scissors, cut a circle out of white paper (about the size of your pizza pan). Get creative and cut designs in the center of the paper like personal names, team names, or initials.
2. Place the stencil on top of the cooled brownie. Once you place the stencil down, do not touch it until you are done.
3. Put powdered sugar into a sifter or strainer. Dust top of stencil with sugar, filling in the design holes. Then carefully lift the stencil straight up off the brownie.

Pizza for Breakfast, Anyone?

If you like pizza all the time, here's a simple, healthy way to have pizza first thing in the morning. These are great when you're in a hurry, but want something other than cereal for breakfast.

INGREDIENTS:

2 English muffins
$\frac{1}{2}$ cup all fruit jam
1 cup grated low-fat mozzarella cheese

TOOLS:

◆ Rolling pin
◆ Baking sheet
◆ Measuring cups & spoons
◆ Butter knife

MAKES 4 PIZZAS!

STEPS:

1. Split English muffins in half by inserting your thumb in the middle and pulling apart the halves. Use a rolling pin to roll them out until muffin halves are flatter and larger circles.

2. Place muffin halves on a baking sheet and lightly toast them under the broiler in the oven or toaster oven.

3. Spread 2 tablespoons jam on each toasted muffin half. Sprinkle $\frac{1}{4}$ cup of grated cheese on top of the jam. Place muffin halves back under broiler until cheese is melted and lightly browned.

TERRIFIC TOPPINGS TO TRY

Flatten English muffins as noted above and try one of these.

- Spread spaghetti sauce and sprinkle with mozzarella cheese.
- Layer turkey slices, some scrambled eggs, and sprinkle with grated cheddar cheese.
- Spread layer of cream cheese, top with peaches, and drizzle with honey.

HONEY

Pizza Pocket

Tuck a few of your favorite toppings inside this to enjoy a hot pizza pocket!

INGREDIENTS:

1 can refrigerated pizza dough
1 tablespoon mustard
$\frac{1}{2}$ pound thinly sliced ham
$3\frac{1}{2}$ ounces sliced pepperoni
1 teaspoon dried Italian seasoning
2 cups grated mozzarella cheese

SERVES
6

TOOLS:

◆ Baking sheet, lightly greased
◆ Knife

Steps:

1. Preheat oven to 425° F.

2. Unroll pizza dough onto baking sheet. Pat dough into a 12-inch square. Spread mustard on dough, leaving only $\frac{1}{2}$ inch at each edge.

3. Layer ham slices and pepperoni down center of dough, leaving $\frac{1}{2}$ inch at bottom and top. Sprinkle with Italian seasoning and cheese.

4. Fold sides of dough over filling, pinching top and bottom to seal.

 5. Bake 20 minutes or until lightly browned. Let cool for 5 minutes before slicing and eating.

Did you know that the largest pizza ever baked (122 feet, 8 inches in diameter) was made at Norwood Hypermarket, Norwood, South Africa, on December 8, 1990? The ingredients included 9,920 pounds of flour, 198 pounds of salt, 3,968 pounds of cheese, and 1,984 pounds of tomato puree.

Simple Pasta Dough

While pre-made pasta of all types is readily available at the store, you will experience a feeling of pride the first time you make your own. Plus, you will be surprised at how simple it is!

INGREDIENTS:

3 large eggs and 1 egg yolk
3 tablespoons olive oil
4 cups of unbleached flour
1 teaspoon salt
$\frac{3}{4}$ cup cold water
Extra flour for dusting

TOOLS:

- Small bowl & fork
- Large mixing bowl
- Large plastic bag
- Clean hands

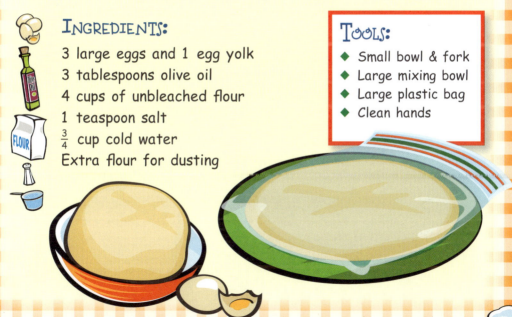

STEPS:

1. Break 3 eggs and separate 1 egg yolk into small bowl. Wash your hands. Beat eggs with fork, then stir in olive oil.

2. Put $3\frac{1}{2}$ cups flour into large bowl and make a deep well in the middle. Pour in salt, then egg and oil mixture from Step 1. With fork, mix in $\frac{3}{4}$ cup water (a little at a time) to keep dough from getting lumpy. When it becomes too stiff to mix with a fork, use your hands to form into a ball. *If at any time dough is too dry, mix in a bit more water or if too sticky, a bit more flour.*

3. Dust work surface with flour and put dough ball on it. Knead dough about 50 times until it becomes silky, soft, and elastic.

4. Put dough into a plastic bag to rest at room temperature for 30 minutes. This is a good time to decide what type of pasta noodles or ravioli you are going to make with your dough. See the following pages. (If you choose ravioli, see page 31 for the yummy filling options!).

Noodle News!

Let's Learn About Pasta Shapes

Spaghetti "Strings" The all-American favorite noodle!

Angel Hair "Fine hairs" Thin & delicate noodles, good with light sauces.

Linguine "Little Tongues" Flat & slippery, good for stir-fry!

Lasagna "Cooking pot" Known for the dish they make; large sheets of pasta used for layering sauce, meat, cheese.

Penne "Small Mustaches" Tubular and tasty for pasta salad!

Rigatoni "Large Grooved" Ridged on the outside to absorb chunky, meaty sauces.

Farfalle, Bow Ties "Butterflies" These are just plain fun to eat.

Ravioli "Little Pillows" Easy to make and fun to fill!

Fusilli "Twisted Spaghetti" Good in baked dishes.

Radiatore "The Radiators" Ridged on the outside, these absorb any sauce!

Macaroni "Dumpling" Best known for Mac n' Cheese.

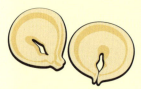

Tortellini "Stuffed Little Hats" Excellent as an appetizer or as a full meal.

Route di Carro "Wagon Wheels" Super in pasta salad and when you are on the go!

Alphabets Learn and eat at the same time; famous for Alphabet Soup.

Making Noodles

It's time to wake up your pasta dough and make some noodles. Before you start, decide what type of noodles from *Noodle News* on pages 27–28 that you'd like to make.

MAKES OODLES OF NOODLES!

INGREDIENTS:

Simple Pasta Dough
  (pages 25 to 26)
Extra flour for dusting

TOOLS:
- Rolling pin
- Clean dishtowel
- Knife

STEPS:

1. Dust a flat work surface and rolling pin with flour.
2. Divide dough into 2 pieces. Cover piece that you are not using with a dishtowel.
3. Roll dough into a large, thin rectangle.

4. With an adult's help, carefully use the knife to cut the dough into long, narrow strips. Re-roll dough scraps and follow the same process in Steps 1–3 until you have oodles of noodles!

MAKING NOODLES USING A PASTA MACHINE

If you have access to one, this is super fun!

1. Tighten pasta machine clamp to table or counter edge.

2. Divide dough into 4 pieces. Cover pieces that you are not using with a dishtowel.

3. Dust pasta rollers with flour and open them to widest setting. Slip one edge of dough between the rollers and crank away. Fold dough in half, flatten edge and run it through the machine again 3–4 times, making the roller narrower on each pass.

4. For linguine, we rolled it at a setting 7 and cut with wide cutting rollers. Add flour if dough gets sticky and cut in two if dough gets too long.

Rockin' Ravioli

Impress your friends by making fun shaped ravioli like circles, hearts, or flowers by using a cookie cutter to cut out pasta.

Ingredients:

Simple Pasta Dough (pages 25-26)

Extra flour for dusting

Small bowl of water

Filling of choice:

❖ Ground beef or turkey, Parmesan cheese, chopped onions

❖ Smoked chicken, grated Monterey jack cheese

❖ Pesto, sun-dried tomatoes, chopped olives

❖ Fresh chopped spinach mixed with ricotta cheese & Parmesan

Tools:

◆ Rolling pin
◆ Knife
◆ Pastry brush
◆ Round ravioli cutter or any simple shaped cookie cutter (about 3")

Makes Dozens of Ravioli!

STEPS:

1. Dust a flat work surface and rolling pin with flour.
2. Divide dough into 2 pieces.
3. Roll dough piece into two rectangles with one for the top slightly bigger. Square off sides using a knife.
4. Lightly brush the bottom piece of dough with water from the small bowl.
5. Place spoonfuls of filling in neat evenly spaced rows leaving about $\frac{3}{4}$ inch free around each spoonful.
6. Lightly brush top dough sheet with water and lay it over the bottom piece with the fillings. Wet outside rectangle sides together, then gently press around each ball of filling to seal the edges.
7. Cut between ravioli with the ravioli cutter or cookie cutter and press edges together again to make sure they are sealed.
8. Re-roll dough scraps and follow the same process in Steps 1–7, until dough is gone!

Cooking Fresh Pasta

The most important thing about making homemade pasta is cooking and eating it fresh—right away!

INGREDIENTS:

8 cups water
Olive oil & salt
Homemade pasta

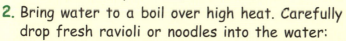

STEPS:

1. Put water into large pot, then add 2 teaspoons olive oil and 2 pinches of salt.

2. Bring water to a boil over high heat. Carefully drop fresh ravioli or noodles into the water:
   — Cook noodles for 1 minute after they float to top.
   — Cook ravioli for 3 minutes after they float to top.

3. Drain pasta in colander and toss with favorite sauce, or butter and Parmesan cheese, and enjoy!

TOOLS:

- Large pot
- Large slotted spoon
- Colander

Im-pastable Word Search

Take a break from cooking. Try to find these words that you learned about! Turn to page 56 for the answers.

Word List

- Macaroni
- Lasagna
- Cooking
- Ziti
- Ravioli
- Pizza
- Calzones
- Chef
- Sauce
- Crust
- Cheese

M	I	T	I	Z	E	R	L	A	N	C	Y
P	A	C	R	U	S	T	F	I	C	A	P
R	E	C	R	U	S	D	I	M	A	L	I
E	I	U	A	N	O	R	P	A	L	Z	Z
S	P	I	N	R	C	H	K	L	Z	O	Z
E	E	W	L	Y	O	E	R	A	O	N	A
E	S	O	K	C	H	N	E	S	N	F	S
H	E	E	T	N	E	D	I	A	E	E	C
C	G	N	I	K	O	O	C	G	S	H	E
C	E	F	S	A	U	C	E	N	T	C	H
I	I	L	O	I	V	A	R	A	T	Y	C

Easy Cheesy Ravioli

These are made quick and easy with wonton wrappers from a grocery store!

SERVES 4

INGREDIENTS:

24 wonton wrappers (usually in the produce section of the grocery store)

4 tablespoons ricotta cheese

2 tablespoons Parmesan cheese, grated

2 tablespoons Mozzarella cheese, grated

8 cups water and pinch of salt

Jar of your favorite pasta sauce

Extra grated Parmesan cheese for topping

TOOLS:

- Square cookie cutter, about 3"
- 2 small bowls
- 1 small spoon
- Large pot
- Cutting board
- Slotted spoon
- Cheese shaker

STEPS:

1. Cut wonton wrappers with cookie cutter.

2. In small bowl, mix together ricotta, Parmesan, and mozzarella cheeses. Place 1 to 2 spoonfuls of cheese mixture into the middle of cut-out wonton wrapper.

3. Add about 1-inch water to another small bowl. With your fingers, dab water around the edges of the bottom wrapper (with the filling on it). Place another wrapper on top and pinch edges together. Continue using the same process from Steps 1–3 until the rest of the wrappers are gone.

4. Warm your favorite pasta sauce.

5. Bring pot of water with a pinch of salt to boil over high heat. Cook ravioli for 3 minutes or until they float to the top. Then remove them with a slotted spoon onto a plate.

6. Serve with your pasta sauce and sprinkle with Parmesan cheese

Likety-Split Layered Lasagna

Need a meal in a hurry? This recipe is so fast that you don't even need to boil the noodles. But watch out, because it'll disappear once it's served!

SERVES 4 HUNGRY PEOPLE

INGREDIENTS:

1 10 oz package frozen spinach, chopped, thawed and drained

$1\frac{1}{2}$ cups ricotta cheese

1 egg white, separate out yolk

Olive oil or vegetable spray

4 cups of your favorite chunky spaghetti sauce

12 no-boil lasagna noodles

$\frac{1}{4}$ cup Parmesan cheese

2 cups mozzarella cheese, shredded

TOOLS:

◆ Mixing bowl & spoon
◆ 8 x 12 inch baking dish, lightly greased

STEPS:

1. Preheat oven to 350°F.

2. In mixing bowl, stir together spinach, ricotta cheese, and egg white.

3. In the order listed, layer the following ingredients in a lightly greased baking dish: 1 cup spaghetti sauce, 4 lasagna noodles, half the spinach mixture, 3 tablespoons Parmesan cheese, $\frac{1}{2}$ cup mozzarella cheese, 1 cup sauce, 4 lasagna noodles, remaining spinach mixture, 3 tablespoons Parmesan cheese, $\frac{1}{2}$ cup mozzarella cheese, 1 cup sauce, 4 lasagna noodles, 1 cup sauce then the rest of Parmesan and mozzarella cheeses.

4. Bake uncovered for about 1 hour or until hot and bubbly. Let lasagna set for 10–15 minutes before serving.

Everything-But-The-Kitchen-Sink Pasta Salad

The more ingredients, the better this salad tastes. So don't leave anything out (except maybe the kitchen sink) and enjoy!

MUST HAVE INGREDIENTS:

8 cups water and pinch of salt

1 pound package fun-shaped pasta

2 tablespoons olive oil

1 tablespoon red or white wine vinegar

$\frac{1}{2}$ teaspoon salt

TOOLS:

- Large pot
- Colander
- Large serving bowl
- Knife
- Measuring cups & spoons
- Small bowl
- Whisk or fork
- Cheese shaker

Optional Ingredients:

2 tablespoons fresh basil, thinly sliced

$\frac{1}{3}$ cup grated Parmesan cheese

$\frac{1}{4}$ cup onion, diced

$\frac{1}{2}$ cup broccoli, chopped

$\frac{1}{2}$ red pepper, diced

$\frac{1}{2}$ cup olives, chopped

$\frac{1}{2}$ hard salami or pepperoni, diced

$\frac{1}{2}$ cup favorite cheese, grated

$\frac{1}{4}$ cup bacon bits

Steps:

1. Bring pot of water with a pinch of salt to a boil. Add pasta and cook until al dente (or for 8–10 minutes). Rinse and drain noodles in colander and transfer to serving bowl.

2. Prepare vegetables and other items that you choose to include and add these to cooked pasta shapes.

3. In small bowl, combine olive oil, wine vinegar, and salt, and mix well with whisk or fork. Pour this dressing over the pasta and toss well. Shake Parmesan cheese on top and chill in the refrigerator before serving. The longer the salad chills, the more the flavors will blend.

Mama Mia Spaghetti And Meatballs

What's more Italian than spaghetti and meatballs? Every chef needs to know how to make this reliable family favorite!

SERVES 4

INGREDIENTS:

For sauce:

1 tablespoon olive oil
$\frac{1}{2}$ small onion, diced
1 clove garlic, minced
2 6-ounce cans tomato paste, plus 2 cans water
1 15-ounce can tomato sauce
$\frac{1}{3}$ cup brown sugar
Italian seasonings to taste

For meatballs:

$\frac{1}{2}$ small onion, diced
1 pound lean ground beef
$\frac{1}{2}$ cup breadcrumbs
$\frac{1}{4}$ cup Parmesan cheese, grated
2 eggs
$\frac{1}{2}$ teaspoon salt

For spaghetti:

1 pound spaghetti noodles
8 cups water and pinch of salt
1 cup Parmesan cheese, grated

Tools:

- Frying pan
- Large saucepan
- Measuring spoons & cups
- Knife
- Large & small spoons
- Medium mixing bowl
- Large pot
- Colander
- Large serving bowl
- Cheese shaker

1. Make the Sauce:
Heat olive oil in frying pan. Add onion and garlic, and sauté until soft. Mix in 2 cans tomato paste and 2 can-fulls water. Add tomato sauce, brown sugar, and Italian seasonings to taste. Let sauce simmer.

2. Make the Meatballs:
Put diced onion, ground beef, breadcrumbs, Parmesan cheese, eggs, and salt in mixing bowl and mix well. Using clean hands, shape into meatballs and add to sauce. Bring sauce and meat-balls to a boil and then simmer for 25 minutes.

3. Make the Spaghetti:
Bring pot of water and a pinch of salt to a boil. Add spaghetti and cook until al dente (for about 8–10 minutes). Rinse and drain noodles in colander and place in serving bowl.

4. Serve sauce and meatballs over spaghetti. Sprinkle with Parmesan cheese and enjoy.

Macaroni & Cheese Please!

We know the kind from a box is yummy, but you'll be surprised by how much better *homemade* mac & cheese is!

INGREDIENTS:

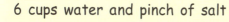

- 6 cups water and pinch of salt
- 8-ounces elbow macaroni
- 2 eggs, separated
- 12-ounces cottage cheese
- 8-ounces sour cream
- 2 cups cheddar cheese, shredded
- $\frac{1}{2}$ cup milk
- 1 teaspoon salt
- $\frac{1}{2}$ teaspoon ground black pepper
- $\frac{1}{4}$ cup breadcrumbs

TOOLS:

- Large pot
- Colander
- Egg separator or small strainer
- Small bowl
- Food processor or blender
- Mixing bowl
- 8-inch square baking dish, greased
- Aluminum foil

STEPS:

1. Preheat oven to 350° F.

2. Bring pot of water with a pinch of salt to a boil over high heat. Add elbow macaroni and cook until al dente (for about 5–7 minutes). Rinse and drain noodles in colander.

3. Separate and save egg whites from yolks in a small bowl. Discard yolks. Wash your hands well.

4. In food processor or blender, add cottage cheese and sour cream. Process until smooth then put in mixing bowl. Add cheddar cheese, milk, salt, pepper, and egg whites.

5. Stir in macaroni and scoop entire mixture into baking dish. Sprinkle top with breadcrumbs. Bake covered with foil for 30 minutes, and then uncover and bake for another 15 minutes. Cool for 10 minutes. Slice, serve, and enjoy!

Great Greek Pasta Salad

Once you try the rich flavors of this salad, you'll want to make it again and again!

INGREDIENTS:

8 cups water and pinch of salt
1 pound pasta shapes of choice
1 pint cherry tomatoes, cut in halves
$\frac{1}{4}$ cup fresh basil leaves, thinly sliced
1 jar Kalamata olives, chopped and pitted
2 cloves garlic, minced
$\frac{1}{2}$ cup feta cheese, crumbled
3 tablespoons olive oil
Salt, pepper, and Italian seasoning to taste

TOOLS:

- Large pot
- Colander
- Large serving bowl
- Large mixing spoon

Steps:

1. Bring pot of water with a pinch of salt to a boil over high heat. Add pasta shapes and cook until al dente (for about 8–10 minutes). Rinse and drain pasta in colander and transfer to serving bowl.

2. Put tomatoes, basil, olives, garlic, and feta cheese in serving bowl with pasta. Combine all ingredients with olive oil and toss. Add salt, pepper, and seasoning to taste. Serve at room temperature or refrigerate. The longer the salad sits, the more the ingredients meld together.

Try for Extra Flavor:

- ◆ Chopped Mint
- ◆ Diced red peppers
- ◆ Garbanzo beans

Baked Wagon Wheel Pasta

The nice thing about a baked pasta dish is that once it's in the oven, you can set a fancy table while it's baking to make the meal extra special.

INGREDIENTS:

8 cups water and pinch of salt
1 pound wagon wheel shaped pasta
2 tablespoons olive oil
1 pound lean ground beef
1 onion, chopped
1 large jar spaghetti sauce
1 cup provolone cheese, grated
1½ cups sour cream
1 cup mozzarella cheese, grated
Grated Parmesan cheese for topping

TOOLS:

◆ Large pot
◆ Colander
◆ Large skillet
◆ 9 x 13 inch baking dish, lightly greased

Steps:

1. Preheat oven to 350° F.

2. Bring large pot of water with a pinch of salt to a boil. Add pasta and cook until al dente, (for about 8–10 minutes). Rinse and drain pasta in colander.

3. In large skillet, heat olive oil over medium-high heat. Add ground beef and onions, and cook until meat is browned, (for about 5 minutes). Then add spaghetti sauce and bring to a boil. Lower heat to a simmer and cook for 15 minutes.

4. Layer in the baking dish: $\frac{1}{2}$ cooked pasta, provolone cheese, sour cream, $\frac{1}{2}$ sauce, remaining pasta, mozzarella cheese, and remaining sauce. Top with Parmesan cheese.

5. Bake for 30 minutes or until cheeses are melted. Serve immediately.

Cheesy Side Sticks

MAKES ABOUT 40 STICKS!

These tasty treats go great with pasta and are a fun afternoon snack, too! They are simple to make thanks to ready-to-use puff pastry sheets found in the freezer section of most grocery stores.

TOOLS:

- Small bowl & spoon
- Measuring spoons
- Rolling pin
- Small microwave-safe bowl
- Pastry brush
- Knife
- Baking sheet

INGREDIENTS:

8 teaspoons Parmesan cheese, grated or shredded if fresh

8 teaspoons Romano cheese, grated or shredded if fresh

Flour for dusting

Frozen puff pastry sheets, thawed for 20 minutes

4 tablespoons butter, melted

STEPS:

1. Preheat oven to 400°F.

2. In small bowl, stir together Parmesan and Romano cheeses.

3. Lightly dust work surface and rolling pin. Using the rolling pin, flatten puff pastry into rectangles or squares.

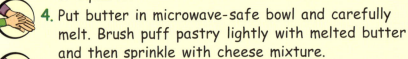

4. Put butter in microwave-safe bowl and carefully melt. Brush puff pastry lightly with melted butter and then sprinkle with cheese mixture.

5. Cut pastry into $\frac{1}{4}$ to $\frac{1}{2}$ inch strips and lay on baking sheet with cheese side up. Bake for 8–12 minutes or until light, golden brown. They will be hot, so let them cool before eating.

Funky Focaccia

Focaccia is funky because it's sorta bread gone flat, sorta pizza, and sorta snack. In any case, you should sorta try it!

MAKES EIGHT 6-INCH ROUNDS OR ONE 11x17 INCH RECTANGLE

INGREDIENTS:

$\frac{1}{4}$ teaspoon sugar

$1\frac{1}{2}$ cups warm water

1 packet active dry yeast—$\frac{1}{4}$ ounce

2 teaspoons salt

4 cups unbleached flour

2 tablespoons olive oil

Extra flour for dusting

Extra olive oil

$\frac{1}{3}$ cup olive oil

2 teaspoons dried rosemary

2 teaspoons dried oregano

Italian seasonings of choice

TOOLS:

- Measuring cup & spoons
- 2 small mixing bowls
- 2 large mixing bowls
- Plastic spatula
- Clean dishtowel
- Rectangle baking sheet with side, lightly greased

STEPS:

1. Preheat oven to 450° F.

2. *Proof the yeast:* To do this, combine sugar and warm water in small bowl, then sprinkle yeast on top. Stir lightly and let stand for 5 minutes or until bubbly.

3. In a lightly oiled large mixing bowl, add yeast mixture, salt, $3\frac{1}{2}$ cups flour, and 2 tablespoons olive oil. Mix together. Gradually add remaining flour until dough clears sides of bowl.

4. Dust flat surface with flour and put out dough. Knead about 50 times to form a smooth, elastic ball. Put dough in second lightly oiled mixing bowl and cover with dishtowel to rise in a warm spot for about 30 minutes.

5. Once dough has risen, press dough into greased baking sheet using your hands. Let stand for 10 minutes to slightly rise again.

6. In second small mixing bowl, combine the $\frac{1}{3}$ cup olive oil, rosemary, oregano, and any other seasonings of choice.

7. Gently press dimples into dough 2 inches apart using your thumb. Drizzle olive oil and seasonings mixture over dimples. Bake for 30 minutes or until golden brown. Serve warm.

Designer Tablecloth

Hosting a pizza or pasta party for friends and family can be a lot of fun, especially when you decorate your own designer tablecloth! Make your tablecloth ahead of time or invite your guests to join in the fun. Let your imagination run wild and be sure to sign and date your masterpiece.

YOU WILL NEED:

- ◆ Lots of newspaper or plastic tarp (it can get messy!)
- ◆ Plain white tablecloth or flat, twin-sized bed sheet
- ◆ Fresh vegetables and fruits cut into fun shapes
- ◆ Knife
- ◆ Washable paints (but if you plan to wash this, use acrylic/fabric paints)
- ◆ Small paper bowls or tin trays
- ◆ Paint brushes & markers

STEPS:

1. Lay out newspaper or a tarp to protect your work area, and then lay your tablecloth over it.

2. Prepare food by cutting everything into shapes or slices. You can even try using cookie cutters to make shapes and create stencils. (If you cut an apple crosswise, the core and seeds appear to be a star, perfect for printing.)

3. Pour paints into bowls or trays.

4. Dip foods into paint and press onto tablecloth or sheet and decorate! Experiment with different colors and shapes. Use markers to turn a corn-cobbed print into the body of a hippo, or use your imagination to make creative drawings. Try a theme tablecloth if you are having a garden tea party or maybe a baseball tea party!

COME COOK WITH US AGAIN!

We hope you had fun in the kitchen! If you accomplished even one of these recipes, you should be proud to know that you made it yourself! And along the way, we hope it was fun and that you made some tasty and yummy eats. Cooking is all about creativity, fun, and trying new foods that you never thought you would.

Don't forget: When you cook, you need to be responsible. This includes cleaning up after you cook and taking care of the things you use while cooking. Please care for the cooking utensils in this package by washing them by hand after each use and then drying them (these tools are <u>not</u> dishwasher safe). Also avoid abrasive cleaning pads.

As a member of the Kids Cooking Club, you can look forward to many more cooking adventures with great new cookbooks on the way! Plus, you will build up your own collection of cooking tools and expertise!

So come on back—we look forward to cooking with you again! Check out <u>www.kidscook.com</u> for additional cooking adventures!

Answer key to the
Im-pastable Word Search

(from page 34)

M	I	T	I	Z	E	R	L	A	N	C	Y
P	A	C	R	U	S	T	F	I	C	A	P
R	E	C	R	U	S	D	I	M	A	L	I
E	I	U	A	N	O	R	P	A	L	Z	Z
S	P	I	N	R	C	H	K	L	Z	O	Z
E	E	W	L	Y	O	E	R	A	O	N	A
E	S	O	K	C	H	N	E	S	N	F	S
H	E	E	T	N	E	D	I	A	E	E	C
C	G	N	I	K	O	O	C	G	S	H	E
C	E	F	S	A	U	C	E	N	T	C	H
I	I	L	O	I	V	A	R	A	T	Y	C

56